WORDS

from the

EAST

WORDS
from the
EAST

Camille Hamilton Adams Helminski

First edition published 2017
by Sweet Lady Press,
an imprint of Threshold Books

© Camille Hamilton Adams Helminski, 1990

Rose illustration and logo design by Cara Helminski

Book design by Daniel Thomas Dyer

All rights reserved. No part of this publication may be reproduced or utilized in any form or by any means, electronic or mechanical, including photocopying, or by any information storage and retrieval system, without prior written permission from Sweet Lady Press.

Library of Congress Cataloging-in-Publication Data

Names: Helminski, Camille Adams, 1951- author.
Title: Words from the East / Camille Hamilton Adams Helminski.
Description: First edition. | Louisville : Threshold Books, 2017.
Identifiers: LCCN 2017028315 | ISBN 9780998125800 (pbk.)
Classification: LCC PS3608.E464 W86 2017 | DDC 811/.6--dc23 LC record available at https://lccn.loc.gov/2017028315

SWEET LADY PRESS
2775 Las Palmas Ave.
Escondido , CA 92025

Dedicated to the One who opens the Way,
with manifold thanks to Dr. Asad Ali,
friend of God

Offered by
Camille

1990

Preface

Dear Reader,

These words come to you as an offering. Flowing through me in the space of several months, they have brought nourishment to me, and I hope will continue to do so for you. A spring bubbled up and began overflowing upon coming into contact with Dr. Asad Ali in Damascus, Syria in May 1990. In the process of opening to Life, and the immanence of God, the reflection of Love became apparent everywhere. Keeping pen in hand helped me to mirror what I saw.

Within each of us is such a well-spring of love and pure water that is just waiting to be tapped; a seed waiting to burst forth into bloom and share its fragrance; a light flickering that is waiting to recognize its kinship with the Sun and so gain new strength and brightness from its Source. These days there are many ways to speak of God... new ways and old ways; but in whatever way we speak, let us be aware that God is nearer than a whisper in our hearts, more naturally present and sustaining than breath, and easy to recognize if we take the time to look. We needn't stretch ourselves too far, craning our necks or twisting our backs—God is already with us. Call and He/She will answer, and the conversation may be the most enlivening you have ever had.

May it rise up through the deepest part of yourself, glowing, shedding light like rain and fireworks. That which is essentially you may burst into song or softly, quietly, begin to brighten, letting thoughts and mannerisms shift to accommodate new In-sights. No seeking is what is sought; coming Home—we have already wandered too far. But it is never too far, or too late, as the Source of Light and Love is always right with us waiting to welcome us and the sooner we turn and listen, the more joy will be ours.

Sit quietly; be empty, and you will be filled; look out at this marvelous creation and see the infinite mirrors of the Face of God. One God, One Source, One Creator enables us to weave ourselves into a glorious pattern of Love; and in moments of darkness or weakness, we do not have far to look to find a light to borrow to re-kindle our own. Such incredible diversity has been given—why? Perhaps so that no matter in what situation we may find ourselves, no matter who or what we are, or what our tastes or yearnings may be, we might find someone or something calling to us, offering us a key to turn the lock on the door of the House of Unity and discover the treasure that is hidden within.

May all we do and are find its roots, its blossom, and its fruit in the secret of Love.

Camille Hamilton Adams Helminski
1990

WORDS FROM THE EAST

Bismillah ArRahman ArRahim

By the morn
and the Light of God
that comes into our hearts,
we are blessed,
surely we are blessed
whenever we open the window
to Divine Soul.

Reflection

When it puts itself
        in the way
        of the Light of God,
even a cement wall
        can reflect the brightness
        for others to see.
Let it hold itself
        in that brightness
that it may continue to reflect
        the power
        of the Almighty God
that inch by inch
it may take on the beauty
        of God's thought.
      "Réfléchir."
Pause, and think,
O you who love the Lord,
that the hardness of your heart,
the darkness of your heart
may turn to Light,
that you may be a beacon
        of radiance
for all to see,
beckoning, calling My people
    to come to Me,
to return to their home.
      "Re"—again and again.
      "Ray", as a drop of sunlight
returns to its source,
returns to its Source
and comes out again,

>   dancing
back and forth;
alive with Love.

(Sealed by circles and lines. Amen.)

Let nothing block the ray of God.
I am ready and willing
for God's Word to be done;
for His Will to flower in me
and spread its fragrance
everywhere, calling
the buzzing bee
who hovers, sips,
>   and flies off
but in doing so makes me
>   more fertile.
I give thanks for those
>   who pollinate
and help to spread the seed
>   of God.

Let there be no blot
>   on this Ray.
Let there be no self-love
>   to block this Way.

Amen.

Humility before God.
Purity before God.
Kneeling in absence of myself
I hesitate to say—
may it be
that only God can
    speak.

Amen.

For His Love
    i offer this,
      i who am no thing,
        no one,
smaller than an ant,
      invisible
before the Face of His Love.
May I disappear
    before His Word.

Amen.

The green man was here.
The curtains took on the color of green
    and moved
with the breath of the wind.
    Thank you

to the "greenness" of Life,
the abundance of Life.
Thank you.

Amen.

Your shining water,
the Sun atop the darkness
and then a patch of turquoise blue
at the edge of the gulf,
    near land—
the place You come to meet us
where we are home,
and remind us
that one day we will be drawn
to our home before time once again.
Back to the center
    on the current of Your Love,
riding the back of a whale,
not swallowed up in its belly,
    but riding high, fresh,
in the clear sun's shine.

We must prepare to go
    back through the needle's eye
to translate for the West
what has been seen in the East.

Trans-late.
To change language,
change tongue,
with which we speak.
New from the root.
Sleeping with pen in hand
that we may awaken
      at the moment of need
and put our pen to work
for His Work,
in service of the Lord.

O Sun, warm my bones,
heal my body;
flush out the impurities
with the strength of your Light.
Let them fall from my fingers, my feet,
and dissolve in your air and earth
without causing any harm.
Purified by You,
irradiate this body
      with Your Love,
cleansing it
that it may be a pure instrument
for performing Your Work.

The breath flows smoothly
like an ocean at peace
with no storm approaching;
swaying back and forth,
gently, softly singing,
and I sleep, the sleep of peace and dreams.

Stop, look, and listen.
In every way
       practice listening to God.
Flex the muscles of the heart
       and mind
that they may grow strong
and energize the body
       to do His Work.

As I am buffeted by You,
help me to be grateful for that, too,
knowing that everything can be a sign,
a Symbol of Your Love,
and that if I look carefully,
I can find the key
to open the treasure
       You are giving to me.

A Change of Atmosphere (The Slap of Glory)

A Slap in His Name:
the mosquito dies and I wake up.
Blood is spilled
but His water washes the world
until it is fresh again.

Darkness and a sense of foreboding
        are dispelled
by the touch of His Light
moving into the heart,
sometimes piercing it with pain
from the brightness of the Ray,
but resurrecting it in Peace,
gently bringing the heart
into a New World.

New Life comes
        as a surprise
things change
        around us
and we change with them.
The seasons run their course
and in spring we wake up
filled with our own beauty,
blossoming through the touch
        of His Hand.
May God bless our new life
        and make it fruitful

that our fruit may bear new trees
to give shade to others
who stand parched in the sun.
For His Mercy and Generosity
are alive forever
and come readily to us
when we open to Him.

Drawings of Life
    are not bought cheaply
    if they are real.
There are many configurations
    to be revealed
    by the Master's touch.
He paints the pictures
    with countless colors;
then we try to decipher the code,
    each as we can,
to reconstruct the puzzle
    in our own way,
that we may share a way to communicate
with those around us
a knowledge of the Truth.
Sometimes it's all so clear
    and comes so easily;
sometimes a fog envelops everything.
Through opening to His Grace
    the veils will fall
and we will learn to paint His Face
    in all ways, for everyone to see.

My days are washed
      by the needs of my children.
Help me to respond to them
      in the right way.
Draw me to You in the Night
      that I may carry the thread
      into the Day
to serve as I am called.
I long to be with You,
to sit, and bask in Your Word,
but the reality is I must pick up
      dishes and socks;
amid the chaos of conflicting demands.
Oh help me to come to You
      in the midst of it all.
Support my bones, my sinews,
      and muscles, that I may move
      with You in my hands,
serving Your song,
the verses You have chosen
for me to enact now.
May I keep knowing that situations change
and that if I keep my aim clear,
the time will come somehow, some way,
to spend every moment's breath with You
in the midst of any struggle,
      to be at Peace,
rocked in Your Word,
      Your handmaiden,
      Your bride,
wrapped in all the wonder
of the wedding day.

Ku, ku,
the mourning dove calls . . .
Where, where is my beloved?
My song can be heard so clearly
    in the pure air
as it rises from my heart
    to my throat
and the call comes again:
where, where is my beloved?
Ku, ku . . .
    "I am here."
His voice answers me in silence
    and comes to my heart,
    full of love,
with blessings to renew my patience,
my strength, and my song;
and from His words
    I gain clarity
and receive the vision of His Presence
    which comes to me
    softly, gently
through the veils of this fine air.
Thank you, O Lord,
for the graciousness of Your giving,
for Your Beauty that I come to see;
O grant that this vision of Your Presence
    may not cease.

        Amen.

La illaha il Allah.
What does it matter
whether you are Christian or Muslim or Jew?
His Name can penetrate your heart
    revealing yourself to you.
Your love is His Love
    ripening in your vessel.
It doesn't matter what name
    you place on it;
it is always His,
    always His.

O Lord,
the beauty of Your creation is incredible!
How did You do it?
Creating such perfection and such loveliness
    with each breath . . .
It is as though Your Breath swirls into shapes
    revealed every moment anew;
in new shapes—each one distinct
    but filled with You.
The blueberry flowers hang full on the branch,
    little bells of nectar
calling the hummingbird to come
    quench his thirst.
His ruby throat glows
    dazzling in the sun,
and iridescent green
    shimmers on his back.
He hovers in praise and thanksgiving

this moment
and helps me to recognize once again
the infinite gifts of Your Grace.

Don't cover your face,
because it's a means of reflection
    of His Light,
    and His Love.
Custom may ask it;
habit may have ingrained it,
but look and listen anew
and open your face
    to His Sight.
Don't hide from Him
    or His people . . .
they need to know, each one,
    each part of the puzzle
    that spells His Name;
so don't hide your face
    from His creation;
don't hide your face
    from His love;
don't hide your face
    from the beauty of reflection
that is possible
when we share in awareness
    of His Purity,
    His Generosity,
    and His Abundant Love.

Breathe, breathe,
>   nourish this body;
>   give it strength.
Lie, or stand, or sit
>   awaiting His Word
and meanwhile breathe.
Inhale His Power,
>   and exhale His Love.

My eyes are wide open.
I can't seem to close them.
I pray that I will continue
to need less sleep.
You came so strongly to my vision
>   dancing in new figures
>   to new music, on new floors.
I thank You for this new sleeplessness;
>   it is odd, strangely unlike
what I have tasted before,
though there is a glimmer,
a shade of older words
that awakened me in the past.
Draw me closer and closer
>   under the covers, the folds
>   of Your meaning.
Enwrap me in the levels
>   of Your consciousness,
that I may be delivered
>   from the tomb
of the ignorant world

and be born again in Your Light.
Let me stand tall in that New World
and hold my arms out as witness
  to the Power and Knowledge
that is my Source,
  and that will come
to all who ask it
if they are willing to give up sleep.

The dawn is coming . . .
  the dark sky begins to lighten
  and I feel Your nearness.
May the false flames that awakened me
be real flames in my heart,
burning up all that is not You.
The dome and tower of Your mosque,
  the local lighthouse calls,
beckoning me to the path of safety.
Help me to follow your call
  to find my place on the rug,
the beautiful carpet of Your Being,
that the birds may sing
at the rightness of all this world . . .
"Wait, and listen," You say . . .
The birds are singing Zhikr
as they wait for the rising of Day.

The rose is of such beauty and such fragrance
that all who see it
come into remembrance
of the original state of glory
at the opening of Creation,
the moment the bud became the rose.
O roses everywhere who open,
in that momentary pause
between two worlds of being,
show us the beauty of maturity
that we may learn from your instruction
how to become fully
      the kind of rose we are;
that we may blend our scents
enlivening and enriching this garden
with the beauty that is of His making,
fulfilling the promise of our birthright
given long before the moment of our birth
when He held us in His Secret
and whispered,
"You are a bud,
      now become the Truth."

Why do mosquito bites and fly bites
      annoy us so much?
Is it because in our independence
      we need more reminders of You . . .
that we don't wander too far
      away from our core?
Continually, You keep calling us,
      "Come near, come nearer to Your Lord."

Everyone thinks they are going to win
when it comes to battles and wars . . .
For some, war is a constant reality
as the struggle for freedom and the shift of ideas
wrecks havoc over their land.
For others war is a distant rumbling
heard in their bellies and their hearts
as food grows scarce and loved ones die
in fields not far from their homes.
The ones who have peace and abundance
often neglect compassion for those who don't
forgetting the harshness and bitterness
of what it must mean
to have one's family ripped apart.

O dear Lord, bring peace,
bring peace to the hearts of men
that they may know You
        deeply and truly
and cease this struggle for power
over those whom only You should rule.

May people begin to listen
        to the projection
of the satellite ray of God,
attuning to God's information
of Beauty and Peace and Love.
Purify our hearts, Lord,
        that we may receive
Your finest transmission,

      attuning our receptors
           to be in harmony
           with Your Word.
Help us then to project it
to help those who are just beginning to hear
           gain reassurance
that they are turning, too,
           to the channel of Your Heart.
Thank You for making human beings
           tools for the projection of Your Love.
Please help us all to reflect it
           until this world
              becomes an even deeper Sea
                  of Your Being
in which we can swim and refresh ourselves,
and light-heartedly play on Your shore
as One family, united in purpose,
in awareness of need, awareness of Love.
Though we have so far to go, Lord,
it could be done in the blink of an eye.
Difficult becomes easy, Lord,
           when You take us into Your side.
May there be Peace,
           but not the peace of oblivion,
the Peace of Knowledge
           and constant mentioning of You,
the One, the Restorer of Unity, the Ever-Living,
the True Life-Giving God.

I come to You
with my arms folded across my heart
and open, dancing

in Your Presence.
Your fire burns in my body.
Your spark has kindled me,
    and I am ablaze—
ablaze with Your Light.
My feet burn against the floor . . .
    may Your fire spread.
Burn us all up in Your Love
'til ash is all that remains.
Then with Your Breath
blow us into nothingness,
the purity of non-existence,
where we may reform,
gathering Your moisture
    into a cloud of being;
then rain us down onto this earth
letting Your thirsty ones absorb You
    through this carrier
that we through Your Grace have become.
No longer is there any barrier.
Your water can flow freely now.

The novacaine numbs my jaw
    so quickly . . .
let it not numb me to You,
but let all that is rotten,
    unsound,
be drilled away,
that only that which is solid and strong
remains, in submission to You.

You have given men and women
the knowledge and skill
to help themselves and each other
care for and restore
this vehicle we ride in
that we may continue our service
and come to know its Source
more and more purely serving
as we learn to hear Your Voice
and move with it each moment,
in manifestation of You,
the One Who Heals,
the One Who Sustains,
the One Who Knows,
the One Who Is . . .
Now, and for all time,
      the only Hu.

The novacaine is wearing off;
may the pain only remind me of You,
burning and purifying my heart.

The sun in the lamp
      tells me Your story . . .
how You have burned with the pain of those You love,
      but through that burning
have helped them to find freedom,
      Oneness with You.

Oh, draw my soul to You,
that I may be of those You love,
burning in Your Abundant Life,
setting fire to all around me
that we may dance together in the flames,

O You, the bringer of Oneness,
      the Joy of my life,
      the One God.

                Amen.

Words pour out
      like water from a fountain;
I am just the rocks
      holding the space
      for it to pool and sparkle
      catching the eye
      of those who may pass,
that they might recognize the opportunity
      to pause and refresh,
      to clean off the dust of the journey
      and fill with new water
      to carry with them
      and quench their thirst;
In His Name,
      the Pure, the Source
      of all sustenance,

increase the purity of these words,
and may more and more people find Your water,
the fountains within each other,
and drink of it as brothers
and as sisters, purely in Your embrace.

It is not the rigidity
        but the open field of Islam
that has nourished me.
I bare my head to Your Sun and Your Sky.
My roof is in ruins,
        the stars twinkle through.
The nightwatchman is going his rounds.

Words come to our ears
        and we hear
        and are able to communicate.
How wonderful!
        that we have the sensitivity
        to know the spoken Word.
"Be still, and know that I am God":
        our inner senses hear as well;
attuned to the fineness of perception
        that need not be so rare.
We all have the power to listen
        in some way . . .
may the ears of our hearts, bodies, and minds

      open to You
      that we all may know
the beautiful music of Your Voice.
      O Lord, Most Fine,
      Most Subtle,
      and yet Most Manifest.

The mountains rise up in praise of You;
the birds soar in Your air;
the flowers burst into bloom
      in the warmth of Your Light . . .
Oh let us see, Lord,
      the miracles You have made . . .
let us rise up out of our flat, dullness
      to respond to Life.
Let us not wait for that moment
when Your mountain of mist
          spews fire
and the wailing of mothers and children
at last wakes us up to You.
Let us come to You, Now,
      when we are able . . .
let us bloom with Your Love,
fresh flowers on the mountainside.

The shades of spring green are so myriad.
The hues of Your palette, endless;
Green—the color of life,

            of healing.
We have arrived at Your door,
            Your threshold.
May we step right foot first
            into Your room.
O Beloved Lord, let me come
        into Your embrace.
Heal me of all inattention
      to Your detail.
Let me become a true lover
      of all that is Real,
           all that is You.

Your cows give milk,
Your sheep give wool,
O Lord, what can I give?
May my words be an offering
to fill someone's need,
        reminding them of You.

The shadows on the road
tell me of my Beloved,
up the hill toward home,
'til at the top, I'm out in the clear,
      in full sun,
out in the open with You.

Your sunlight falls across my lap
        and gently awakens me . . .
as I look up into the fronds of the palm,
Your sunlight dances there, too.
You call so consistently,
        opening my heart and mind
        to Your soft beckoning.
"I am here," You say,
"Come, awaken to this day.
 Come, rise out of your bed,
        and walk with Me . . .
Holding My Hand, let Me lead you."
Who's speaking?
It's Your Voice coming through
        this person,
        this point of existence
        through Your Love.
O thank You, Lord,
        for awareness of Your Presence,
        for Your Voice,
        for Your abundant Generosity.
Thank You, and again, thank You.
Extend my purity
        that I may be empty of my small self,
        and listen only to You,
standing upright,
in the fullness of the Light that is my strength.

Muhammad, you are as an oasis
>in the desert of many lives,
>a place of refuge
>>and refreshment
where weary souls may rest
>>and be renewed
receiving guidance inwardly
>for the long journey ahead,
hearing the Voice of God
>through the Holy Quran
which came in a single night
>and was subsequently revealed
that all those thirsting in the desert
might rise up and be healed,
>healed from doubt,
>healed from ignorance,
>healed from loneliness and pain,
fed by the holy bread
>of the Holy Word of God.
The simplicity of the message,
>and yet its wideness and detail
support our tired ears
>perking them up that they may say,
"Oh, yes,
>this is something to which I must listen.
Let me hear these words;
let their meaning sink deeply into me
that I may know
>and be alert
and listen to the Will of God,
>that I may do my part
>to bring His Will to fruition
>restoring the desert of many hearts,

healing this land of His Making,
restoring its beauty that men have disturbed."
O Muhammad, peace and blessings be upon you . . .
thank you for bringing His Word.
And thanks, abundant thanks be to You,
    O Lord Most High
for letting Your Source run through,
    not cutting us off,
    not abandoning us,
but offering us, ever anew,
    Your water
that we may be filled with that which is pure,
    and return,
    ever again return,
        to You.

Your sunlight dances like a flame
    on my kitchen floor.
May it bless and enliven this place
where we cook,
where friends and family gather
    to eat Your food
and share in Your abundance,
    O Nourisher,
    O Sustainer of Life . . .
May those who hunger everywhere,
    in Africa,
    around the world,
    and in our cities here,
be fed, be fed most beautifully

by the Hand that reaches out to them
        serving them with your Love.
May Your Spirit shine in them
        dusting off the outer dirt,
bringing them wholly into yourself,
that they may hunger no more
but trust in Your Abundance,
        Your Generosity and Your Care,
        O Lord of All Worlds.

Your sweet water
        flows down my throat
        into my belly,
and gives me strength,
        renewed vigor
to face the task ahead;
may it bring me clarity as well
        washing me from the inside
spreading out through arteries
        to every remote corner of this body
bringing light and energy,
        turning on receptors in every cell
that I may know Your Voice, Your Will
        with every particle within which
        You have given me to live,
that through living I may manifest You,
walking with Your Breath
        upon my face,
breathed in the fire of Your Light,

O You, the Creator of Life,
the One Source,
the One God.

When we first came here,
    the elm tree was standing
    tall and regal,
spreading its branches wide,
calling to the birds and the sky,
voicing Your Greenness
    at the edge of the forest.
It wasn't long though before disease caught it
    and it died,
but its ghost stood still,
too tough to be felled,
yet a home for friends of the sky,
    it waited.
Year by year its branches bent lower,
until it became an upside down reflection
    of its former self—
long bony fingers reached
    almost to the ground.
Alone in its whiteness
    it stood among the green,
a spectre at halloween;
then, piece by piece
    it began to fall,
first smaller branches,
    then larger,

until the trunk alone kept hold of the place
in which it had chosen to grow.
At last, this year
      with a loud crash in the night
      the elm tree fell to the field
lying in rubble at Your feet.
Fairies still dance
among its bones on moonlit
      nights, I'm sure,
      and tell tales of its
      once stately presence
in this green world.
Oh may the stories
they tell of us when we pass
be as good—
      that we lived and died
nobly, in service
to this field of Being
which You have sown,
      O Maker of Visions,
      and of Truth
      and of Strong Reality,
      the One God
in whom we all live
and gain our greenness.
Thank You, O Lord, for the bestowal of Life.
May we put it to good use.

The stars were out when I awoke
      now they've vanished in Your Light.
The line of trees has become

      visible on Your hill,
and standing high,
one tree alone
      with its smaller neighbor
dances strongly in Your wind.
Thank You for this dance, Lord
and for letting me share it
with the green man
      who is my friend.

O Lord, refresh Your Word in me.
Increase the subtleness of my hearing and my sight,
and the fineness of my expression.
Enrich it with Your Voice.
I do not know if what comes from me
      will be accepted as currency,
      words for circulation,
but that is not for me to know,
      but only to voice what is given,
pulling from a constantly subtler space,
bringing a sound of You, here.
Please Lord, accept my prayer.
I am nothing,
      but a vessel for You.
Fill me with Your Love
and let it pour over the sides
      and out every cell
that nothing may be in separation
      from Your Love,
O Lord, Most Immanent.

I, a mother, come to You
      kneeling,
      softly calling
           You
to come quickly to me
      with Your blessing
      and protect my children
      from any harm
      that might truly harm them.
That they might sometimes be battered
      by the storms of life,
      I understand,
but keep them from permanent harm,
      let them move with Your Radiance,
      let them sense Your Will,
           Your Plan,
      and dance and work to fulfill it;
let them sow Your seeds.
Let them plant vineyards and orchards,
let them grow many flowers . . .
      for generations . . .
and also, O You Who are All-Knowing,
      feed them Your Knowledge,
that they may bring new benefit
      to this old world—
innovating new solutions
      to difficulties here.
Let them shine among men and women
      that others may be lit by their fire;
always two logs burn better than one,
keeping each other aflame.
Oh may mothers everywhere
      teach their children of Your Love,

>   Your Generosity
>   and Your Care,
> that each new generation
>   may spread Your Light farther
>   and deeper,
>   and higher.
> "I asked for one kiss,
>   You gave me six" . . .
> may the worlds be filled with You,
>   apparently.
> May You flow more and more into our existence,
> and may we and our children
>   flow more and more from and into You.

> Why am I so cold, Lord?
> Nestle me in Your heart
> that I may burn and warm myself and others—
> healing us with Your heat.

> Most flowers have five petals,
>   though forget-me-nots,
>   pansies and lilacs have four
>   and tulips, six.
> Varied are Your numbers,
>   but pattern underlies,
>   creating Beauty in Order
> that we may see and surmise

   that Order is Beautiful . . .
Oh may we bring order to our lives
   that beauty may blossom from it
   to make fragrant our world.
Five points on a star,
   though sometimes six are drawn;
when there are only four,
   it becomes a cross,
an indication of our path with God,
   and for men and women,
   up and out.
Interphased with five,
   we become nine,
   complete radiance,
a sun within this universe.

Today, I feel rather like a lump of ash,
as though if You or almost anyone
   might blow on me,
I would disappear
     into the wind.
Exhaustion severs my mind and my feelings
   from my body
   and it lies adrift
in loose flecks upon the ground.
Yet, I know that if You call me,
   everything would open up at once
and body, feelings, thoughts
   would realign
inoculated by Your Voice,

rising up to serve,
    indestructible with Your Care.
A single sound of You,
    can call me right back to myself
and I will stand
    and open my arms
        to Your world,
ready, listening for the slightest rustle of need
for which You have awakened me
    to be Your hands to fill.
Wherever I can soothe or heal
    in Your Name,
let me be there.
Let me have the strength
    to suffer and to bear
whatever comes to me
    as a gift from You,
knowing that each experience
    enriches my ability
to be a Human Being
    and to share
the knowledge of Your Presence
        everywhere.

This world is a tomb.
    Help me out of this old world
    into Your land;
a new level
    filled with new views
where Your Voice can always be heard.

Don't let me lose sight
      of Your Face, Lord.
Allah, there is nothing else.
Without You,
      I cannot go on.
Please point the way—
      expand each moment
      until I can see . . .
Sustain the notes
      until I can hear.
Every moment You are new—
      I do not want to waste
          any part of You,
and yet I see
      how easily somehow
      I can let You slip away.
O Lord, cultivate gratitude
      in my heart
and patience in my mind
and resilience in my body
that I may rise to You
throwing out the ballast
      of ingratitude,
      impatience,
      and lethargy.
Help me to lighten my existence
      Lord,
that I may dance
      less heavily
      upon this earth,
disturbing less of Your Creation,
bringing more of You into manifestation,
      brightening,
      that You may be seen.

What are we to do, Lord?
Perhaps in writing,
    I can find an answer . . .
You have given us a family;
they need food—
    food for thought,
    and heart, and body,
so we need to pursue a livelihood,
but in which direction do we turn?—
    from East to West, or West to East?
The Eastern world writes
    from east to west,
    from right to left,
counteracting gravity and logicality.
In the West, we write
    from west to east,
    from left to right,
ordering our steps scientifically;
no wonder the east is far more prone to poetry,
more receptive to the subtleness of language
    and the word.
The West gets caught in the concreteness
    of its thoughts.
How can we make "DOG"
    become "GOD"—
the simplest things can hold a key,
but we discount them—
    just unimportant insights—
    not related they say,
    but without them,
who would have discovered relativity?
What now am I not seeing?
What key is not recognized?

Let me move backwards
        in my mind
        that I may realize,
open to everything,
        but not running away—
Please Lord, help me to see,
        and to say
        the Truth.

Even the sharpest knife
doesn't stay sharp forever.
One must rub it against stone.
A dull knife
        cuts nothing well,
and accidents do happen.

Your snow-capped mountains, Lord,
        are so clear and so cold.
High above the worldly world they tower,
        tall statements of Your Power.
They watch so pointedly,
        all our misdeeds and good pursuits,
        but without judging;
watching silently they wait
        holding their knowledge
        in the secret of stone.
For eons they have waited . . .

how many more years will pass
until You ask for the stories,
the tales of our lives
    they hold inscribed
        in their crevices and rocks?
May it be that when that time comes,
    men and women will have learned
to garner their actions into Your basket,
    leaving aside the unpure,
anything through which they lose the intention
    of bearing Your fruit.
Oh, may the mountains echo
    with the purity of will,
witnessing man's strength and fineness
    in fulfillment of the covenant
    You gave him long ago.
May it be that we carry out Your will
    and magnify Your Creation here below.

The ants and the wasps cluster thickly
    at the top of the peony plants,
called by the buds' sweetness,
    even though they are still closed.
How do they know the nectar is there
    before the blossom?
Some instinct leads them
    straight to their goal.
O lead us Lord, to Your sweetness
    and sweeten us with Your Word,
that though we may not have fully blossomed,

others may find Your food,
some sweetness to sweeten their ear,
that everywhere Your nectar may flow with abundance
drawing us close to You.

The persistent poverty project—
words lying on a file;
whose poverty is persistent?
Why need it be?
We bring our bowls before You, Lord.
Oh fill them quickly
that we may run
with the swiftness of Your wind
to fill those empty bowls
and hearts
who persistently project their need.
Oh lend us swiftness,
and lend us food . . .
We owe everything to You . . .
You who charge no interest,
but give us interest instead
for every step we take toward You.
It is You who wants to fill those bowls,
You who are the Source
for the knowledge of calling,
and the answer that comes—
You are both.

The water in the river ripples
    nestled effortlessly within Your breath;
the trees shade the river's side,
    standing guard,
waiting to provide refuge
    for anyone who comes to them.
The greenness of Your Glory
    is a sight to see!
Each branch, a new expanse,
each leaf, a whole world.
O wrap us in Your Glory, Lord;
    make our eyes to see.
Let us know that You are watching,
    waiting,
for our boats to turn toward You,
    guided by Your Love,
        Your abundant Love.

The evening is drawing to a close,
    what words do You wish to say?
I will listen,
I will listen . . .
It is such sweet music,
    that my pen falls idle;
such sweet music,
    that I am absorbed
into the sound,
into the waves of Your Presence,
        Hu.
Tune my ears.

      Oh, tune my heart,
oh, please make me an instrument
      to accompany Your Voice.
O sweetest of all Musicians,
sing,
    sing
    through me.

Children,
    children are such a gift,
  and yet such a demand—
sometimes they keep me going,
and sometimes they keep me from going.
They hold onto me,
    and keep me holding on
        to concrete reality,
trying to satisfy their needs.
But what do they really need?
    Companionship;
    a focus for creativity,
    ways for love and food-ideas
        to be brought into being.
They are hungry as I am
    for ways to be in this world . . .
Maybe together
    we can discover
new ways
    of Being and doing.

The ants still congregate
    in the middle of the night
and the fish thinks it's still day
    because no one turned off the light.
Even in the depths,
    they continue to swim
from hour to hour
    resting for only moments in between.
We can move from our to Our
when we wake up
    in between the swishes of our wishes
that always drive us onward
    into the night.
Let's forget to turn the light off
rather than neglecting to turn it on.
Let the light inside us shine
    as though it were day
illuminating the depths inside
    our hearts.
Don't let us swim away
    from the Light that is You
to hide in the dark in the rocks.
Help us to let go of fear,
    and frolic in the dappled light
    of Your Sunlit world,
    even in the depths.
Even in the darkest hour—
don't let the minutes flee
without bringing You to flower
    on the surface,
a large translucent lotus,
    fragrant and apparent,
whose roots dangle down

   into our center
and draw our being up,
   into the Beauty of Your blossoming.

A plant of varicolored leaves,
  waving in the breeze
    looks on
while overhead the fan turns,
  turning the light's shadows
'til the plant dances in strobe,
vibrating so fast,
  it almost disappears . . .
So bright with Life
  it quickly passes
from one split-second to the next . . .
Breathing Life,
  it says,
"I'm here,
  I live.
 You can, too."

O Lord, wrap Your cloak of Grace around me.
  Come softly to my door.
I am ready and waiting for You
  to quietly enter in . . .
  there is a place prepared.
A fire is burning in the hearth,

and supper is laid.
O, my beloved, come and dine with me,
      upon the feast that You have made . . .
Such luscious fruits and varied textures
      will end our meal,
but linger, always linger,
      stay with me, do not leave.
Without You, I can do nothing—
      I cannot rest, I cannot sleep,
I cannot begin to meet the day.
O Lord, stay close beside me,
      do not let me turn away.

It's not even really a road,
      it's more of a way,
not much traveled, old,
with holes it's easy to fall into
unless you look down and ahead.
Help me to be patient, Lord.
There are seas of words
      seething inside,
longing to come out—
      out into the air.
Help me to find the proper place,
the right way
      to voice them into space
where they can be heard,
and I can see them stand alone
to pass on to one
      who may need them,

children of Your inspiration,
       and my hands
and this heart You gave me.
Oh, help me find the way;
the ancient way
       well-traveled,
but with new steps I walk
as a baby,
       just learning.
I stumble . . .
help me to rise,
strengthen my bones,
my balance, and my sight—
Guide me, Lord,
       and as a dear friend of Yours, Ali,
I ask, "Accept my prayer."

A parking lot behind a complex of stores—
people coming and going,
a busy afternoon . . .
short tempers, a few smiles,
and many blank faces . . .
Is anyone thinking of You?
At this moment,
       who has You in mind?
Is it the man in the truck,
or the lady in the Peugeot?
Or the mother with two toddlers,
facing shopping with tantrums,
where does she locate her courage?

Where do they all look?
Where do they find what they seek?
You are the one shop
      where we can all be satisfied . . .
but who looks up to see,
to notice the sign over the door:
"Come in, all welcome,
      services free."
Just offer your heart,
offer your life,
and the One behind the Counter
will satisfy your every and only need.

"Oh listen, all you gentle people,
      and you rough ones as well . . .
you have been given warning
      so many times,
and though the seasons pass
      before your eyes,
you still wonder,
      and wander
      far from your home."
I, too, get lost between the pages
      of the Good Words
      that have come down;
but stop on one page,
      look and take heed.
Read, read, and listen . . .
      the Truth is there;
out of each letter it oozes,

      each punctuation point.
So fertile is the power of the Word
      that all of this creation
could in seven days become apparent
though millions of years pass
      and still we don't grow clear enough
      to purely reflect "Be",
because, because . . .
      we linger at the doorstep,
      we forget to bow,
drawn astray by each dancing breeze
      we forget the straight path.
Every hour, may we restore our honor
      and our place,
      learning to re-create
      our own existence
through listening,
      purely listening to Your Word.
The Word of God has been given
      in so many ways,
      so many times . . .
how can we be so deaf?!
O God, crack the shell
      of our indifference,
loose the shackles of our fear,
guide the boats of our existence
      home into ourselves,
      into the port,
      the most secure harbor that is You.

The bunny's ears are veined
	like hibiscus,
		like Althea, rose of Bethlehem,
finely fashioned and upright,
		arched out to catch your Voice.
Softly both move,
	in silence,
so as not to miss a word
	of Your making
by risk of overlaying a false sound.
Oh may we be as quiet
	in Your Presence
and as alert,
but when we hear,
	let us stand up and rejoice!
Singing praises
	and thanksgiving,
and as the one You loved so much,
	in Bethlehem,
		then and now,
let us use what You have given
to call others to Your embrace
that more and more and more may see
		and know Your Face.

The beauty bush is full now.
It has come into "pinkness"
		gradually,
changing softly, breathing imperceptibly
from green to pale blush to full blossoming

     abundant Pink.
The tiger swallowtails,
  delighted, dance,
flitting from blossom cluster
    to throng
together abundantly on the bush
that looks like one,
  but is really two,
arching together over the cellar door.
From the deck above,
   the branches interweave
    until one presence is apparent,
    one abundance is perceived,
and all the air around
   is perfumed with the fragrance
    of their unity.

Lavender and pink . . .
  why do they go so well together?
Because they share red . . .
  the same current flows in their veins,
  the same tone harmonizes the eye
and from lavender to purple,
  we gain blue
    and the sky
in all its glory
  leans down to me to say,
"Would that you could see me
  in the Day beyond day . . .
when I in even greater glory

                shine,
wrapping the earth and all existence
            in my arms,
bringing the truest green to light."
"My eyes, my eyes are blue," you say . . .
"Yes, and they will see . . .
            they will see . . .
            the dawning of the Day."

For brown eyes, too

Eyes of every color
            hold the light;
magically reflect the image
            upside down
and send a message to the brain
            to translate,
but sometimes messages get crossed,
            and synapses balk.
The brain misfunctions
            along the lines
            of old awarenesses and words
ingrained by antique voices
            of dubious accuracy,
            mildew and lace,
            or beer and barley . . .
Open the window!
            Quick,
            open the door!
Let the eyes have a new chance—

        uncross those lines.
Let the vibrations pour
     into the brain—
     Let it rain
impressions, glorious impressions
free of distracting restrictions . . .
       Let the eyes soar
carrying the mind
     on wings of new vision.
Oh, let it pour,
    let it pour,
        let it pour,
a veritable deluge of light.
O God, bring us new sight!

It's not an ordinary road,
     this rubbled path
down which I walk;
     ancient stones, from somewhere,
mark its face.
      Sunk in shallow pools of water
around which one must pass,
     the surface rolls . . .
uneven passage, not a smooth
     highway quickly left,
this road could be anywhere
behind forgotten city walls
     down narrow darkened lanes
midst palm trees, olives, or bougainvillea
out into the sun . . .

yet here it is,
    here am I,
in Brattleboro, Vermont—the USA.
Even here, ancient and sacred voices can be heard.
Even here the numinous can touch us,
even in this often senseless Western world
that is so saturated
with sensuality
    that openings become blocked
and we forget Reality;
the Reality of a simple road
    leading through water and sun
    open to the roof of heaven
    drawing us on,
        on,
    to the Place of the Placeless,
    to the One goal
which in the end we all seek,
    or too late come to find . . .
the one existence,
the one path
that turns us inside out
    that we may become the dust
to cushion someone else's feet
        through Love.

I still have so much to learn
    about how to interact . . .
when to speak
    and when to not

voice what to whom . . .
Help me see, Lord,
      the nuances
of Co-munication,
how to dance the dance
      of language
so that I don't step on any toes.

Another iris opens
      as the older fleur fades—
the changing of the guard
      from French to English
across the channel of life's breath
      into non-existence . . .
The petals fold upon themselves,
      the "tissu" shrivels
      into a tight pocket
      of damp enfolded darkness;
the life moves back into the seed,
      a new seed though
      life makes in death,
drawing all the beauty and the fragrance
      each flower has known
down,
      down,
            into the womb,
the birthing place of those who follow:
Nature's laboratory
      for the next generation
where hidden from the light of worlds,

        in mysterious darkness
she weaves the molecules of life,
tying new patterns
        into her fabric
as moment by moment
the seed swells into existence
        and bursts forth
into the fertility of Earth
who hides the seed in her own darkness
until the moment comes
        when up, out of that darkness
the seed sends forth her arms
pulling the promise of her dress
        up through her stalk
to stand and bend in the sunlight
        and the gentle rain,
waiting, hoping for that moment
when Nature's promise is fulfilled
and in all her glory,
        the new bud unfolds,
spreading her skirt wide
to catch the glance
        of all who sense
and welcome her presence here . . .
        A new flower has come!
        A new opening shows forth—
the presence we all carry inside,
Lord, don't let it hide,
        or be afraid;
let each fragrant fragile bloom
        stand strong,
        full of pride in You.
Let no self-thought linger,

but only let there be
      Your fragrance,
           and our humility.

The sheep have been moved—
a new pasture across the road.
Already the grass
      has been trampled,
but between the arms
      of the old elm
whose branches fell
      from age,
they lie together
      in the shade
of the remaining trees
      and speak softly
           to each other,
inaudibly, to our ears,
sharing the Word of Contentment:
the knowledge
      that You are near.

"The raiment of righteousness,
      that is the best."
That is the clothing
      with which we are blessed . . .
let us not leave it folded on shelves,

or hanging unused in the closet
> where moths may dismantle it

so that when we remember
> it is too late . . .

let us call for that raiment now.
Let us wash and perfume ourselves
> with His Water and Fragrance,

and piece by piece
> slip over our heads

the clothes made by the hands
> of righteousness,

that we may stand in His Glory,
> in His ranks,

in attendance at His Court,
where the sweetest music
> calls us to dance,

and weave the patterns of His Voice.

You have rhythms and ways,
> O Lord,

that are constantly moving.
Your abundance flows so quickly,
that no two moments ever are the same.
Help me to be a fish in Your waters,
> responsive to the current

that I may sooner find
> my breeding ground.

Let me swim,
> free of encumbering clothes,
> bared to Your motion,

letting it guide me to the Source.
As I move upstream, help me to breed in the shallows
    where my children may
    more easily come to life,
but then pull me
    back to the depths
where I may swim free,
    letting Your Light
    shine on my smooth skin
        and reflect into the sky
as I leap with joy into the air,
    but always, always,
diving, returning into You,
the Ocean, who are my home.

Locust petals everywhere
    thickly fallen to the earth
and winging gently, softly
    through the air
to land in among my hair,
brushing my shoulders
    and the branches,
down, onto the ground.
Such fertility and sweet sense
    of breath upon the air
carried into planting
to prolong and renew.
Tree spirit voices sing
shedding happy tears
    like rain—

small pea blossoms,
bringing nourishment to our hearts,
and grandchildren to the soil.

Mary,
words came for you in the night.
In my sleep, your gentle voice spoke
reminding me of your being, your presence,
and the softness of your voice;
yet within it, such strength lives,
such depth of feeling has no floor,
but endless as the waters,
your love flows out of you
into our hearts
to comfort and to nurture
      as we each may need—
you stretch out your hands
      and your heart
           to feed
all the people, everywhere,
      as you did your son,
with the love of God,
      and the knowledge of the One,
the Totality of Beingness
      that lives
within, without, and through
each and every one of us
      as we turn
to look at you,
      and through you

see His/Her Face . . .
    God,
who truly has no gender
    but is the impulse
        and fruition
of every seed,
    no matter what the name.

Morning is awakening—
bird voices fill the air.
The window is reflected on the floor;
Light can make patterns show up anywhere.
Within each pane a whole world dwells.
Now the carpet's edge floods with light
and red and white and blue shine bright,
    each thread glistening
    while just an inch away,
the fibers lie still in the dark
waiting to be revealed
    as living patterns, too.
The hands that wove these knots,
where are they?
Do they yet linger in the light,
dancing back and forth across the warp,
or are they gnarled and rough,
too stiff to move so finely now?
Perhaps already they lie still
at rest in the earth's cave,
returned to the darkness of the womb of the grave.
Quickly though, they may have risen
to grasp threads of Sunbeams, moonbeams,

   and starlight,
weaving the finest cloth
  to toss
  down to clothe us
  in Beautiful Remembrance;
encouraging our hands to weave His Light
into new patterns for this waiting world.

Two cats howling in the night
  awaken my daughter.
She fears for the bunny
  that is already dead.
The body remembers
but morning will be here soon
and memory of this awakening
will become a dim thought.
The first bird begins to sing:
  Allah Hu
  Allah Hu . . .
  Allah
  Allah:
a sweeter sound soothes us.
The body remembers;
may it remember the love.

You move so quickly
  that I lose You
when I don't make space to pray.

The crow calls early, "Allah, Al-lah."
What country have I been in?
Where did I lose my way?
I can just see Your green horizon
      hovering at the edge of the hill.
Help me to climb back up
      to Your vantage point
that I may survey
      all these lands,
      knowing each one,
but not be entangled anywhere.
The mist rises,
      then with a breath
      it is dispelled.
May a good charm be cast;
may I hold Your Name as my talisman,
guarding me from falling away
      into the pit of doubt,
and if by chance, in a moment,
      I forget and slip into blackness,
may Your Name help to pull me out,
      bringing me back to the hill of sunrise
      and Light.

"Tell My people
this world is a reflection for them
      of My Voice,
vibration made visible . . .
'Be' and the world began.
Humanity suffers in separation . . .

draw back the veil.
Be still, and know that I am God;
then look,
then listen, then taste
      with the whole of yourself
and every impulse you receive
      will be the Name of God."

O Lord, give me energy;
let it fill my veins
that I may do
      that which awaits me here.
I cannot stay on Your mountaintop.
Needs clamor
      and order must be served—
Oh guide my hands, Lord,
      and gird my bones
        with Your muscle and sinew.
Strengthen my soul, Lord,
      that I may be in this world,
and yet be only with You.

The heat of this day
      warms my heart,
O my Soul,
O my Beloved.
One can hear the snap of a twig

        ripple through the air.
Machines drone Your Name
        and the winds carry it farther,
        lifting it through treetops
        and glancing it upon the grass,
chanting it through forests
        and into this clearing
where they pause
        and Your Name comes to rest
here upon this carpet of green
where Your abundance bubbles up
in a new fountain fresh
        with Your giving
        and Your sparkling graciousness.
I can see a rainbow
        glistening in Your spray
            hovering,
in promise of color and light,
in declaration of the facets of creation
that will spread with each drop
        of water,
flying to each corner of this clearing,
borne on the back of the wind—
that no part of Your Greenness may wither,
but that each blade of grass
        may strengthen its roots
and stretch higher
            into Your atmosphere.

One rhododendron flower
uniquely pink amidst the green:
leaf fingers stretching in all directions,
touching the Unseen—
catching food there,
transferring it down liquid passages
to roots holding stable in the earth
who know the secret
and can send the message of flowering
      to this one bud.
In just a moment,
      it will open
        smiling,
passing kisses to the air,
and glimpses of the future
      to those steady roots.

The young swallow preens her feathers
      in the light,
then rests in the warmth
      of this new sun,
heart rocking her body
as she waits,
watching, on the railing,
as brothers and sisters dash off into space.
The brown cow-bird calls encouragement,
when in a fraction of a moment,
this swallow-child, too, leaps,
      and split-fire brisks off
           into other air and wing worlds.

This is the time of Bestowal—
      the early morning,
when all is still
and inner voices can be heard
      inside myself
and from the inside of everything
      that shares this world.
Bird voices are easy to hear,
but plants as well, have their song.
The shrimp plant vibrates words:
"With water and food, I will flourish;
oh, don't you love the dawn!
I dance in it every morning
and am so grateful it has come,
for my flowers gain their rosiness
from the bright light of the sun.
I need the light to be fully what I am;
what I have the promise to be.
Some ants crawl upon my back;
      they like my sandy soil.
New soil would refresh me.
With care, I can live
      a good long while;
I can be a companion;
I, too, can speak,
for at the moment of our birth,
by our God-mother,
we each were given the gift of speech."

Al-Judi Mount . . .
Now I have told you what it signifies—
the pain, the difficulties,
but the vision
of all that's possible for man
when he listens and obeys
the word of God
that comes into his soul
and is known by his heart—
the smallest finger of God
with which we can hold on
  and pull all of Him inside,
  lighting His hugeness up wide
  inside ourselves.
Al-Judi Mount—
  let us remember
that we may be one of Noah's true family
  and not perish outside the ark.
The olive branch awaits us—
  peace and stability
  on God's mountain,
with access to the fertility
  of His valleys that lie below.

Bismillah ArRahman ArRahim.
Muhammad, peace and blessings be upon you,
you are the full moon
who reflects so much of the light of the Sun.
If Jesus had lived thirty years longer
  in public life . . .

this, you did.
You gave us examples, and Ali as well,
and your daughters and your wives
of how we might learn to mold our lives
        to better catch His Light
and let it bounce
back into the air
to create a shining fabric of our deeds
that will cover us with glory when we die
and lend a brightness to this world
that more may see
to find the path
out of whatever dark hole
they may have dug
        and come to stand tall
on the surface of this earth
with arms outstretched wide
            and head thrown back
absorbing the brilliance of the heavens
        into their hearts
and letting it open, mirroring
the expansion that is beyond
        our knowing.

I awaken to this warm womb,
        and nestle into this small world
where everything is provided
and I am at rest in the security
        of this moment.
Breath rocks me,

   and I trust this water
   that brings me air.
Sound filters through,
   distant songs and presences
touching my heart,
   and helping me to grow,
and I find the time has come—
   don't lock the door—
I do need to pass through
     into a wider world,
a world of Light and Brightness
I can just begin to feel.
My birthday is approaching;
I can feel myself stretch long
   reaching for the opening—
head first, then hands, then feet
and a flash,
   a burst of breath;
and I am free,
   slipping gratefully
     into the arms of the Mother
   who has been waiting for me.

O Mother,
I come into your presence,
and my reflection fits so well,
as one hand is enfolded
   in the grasp of the other.
I hold your hand,
and you hold mine

and strength passes,
        back and forth,
        between us.
I feel your support,
and you feel my love.
There are no barriers
        to giving,
for naturally, by osmosis
        you have fed me,
and feed me still.
Invisible pathways
        still exist;
no connection has been lost.
Invisible bread
        keeps flowing
from your heart,
        to mine,
and I receive
and grow strong . . .
that one day, I may walk out
        into this world
trailing your fragrance and presence
within and behind me,
and open in marriage with Love,
        to the child
who will come to my womb,
and hold the hand of my heart.

I live in two worlds
        at once,
and through their relation,

come to understand myself.
Bound in double being,
    I exist—
rooted in this earthly soil,
    but simultaneously
my mirror-side envelops me
    embracing me in space.
Together we tumble
    through the passage
    of day and night,
helping each other
    to see the other's service
and to blend
until in one moment
    coalescence occurs
and melded into Oneness
    a molten heart is formed
    and disappears.

The new geranium
    peeks around the corner of the door
    to say hello . . .
    good morning greetings.
Rain-bird voices call
and red-winged blackbirds perch
    at the top of the tall grass.
It bends a bit but holds.
Such a slender stalk supports weight.
May I like-wise support more
    in this world,
with the help of Nature's mystery,
    not just the strength I sometimes call my own.

Allah! There is no God but He.
Open the window to His Words,
    and you will know.
There is only He, She, It—
    it doesn't matter what the name;
there is only One.
    Source of Life,
    Source of Love and Peace,
Namer of the Named,
    the only Victor,
    the only Defense,
the Owner of All Worlds,
the Sole Appointer of Recompense,
the Merciful, the Generous,
    and the Good,
the Everlasting Not Created One,
to You I render homage,
    to You I render praise.
Help me, guide me,
You who know all ways
    known and unseen.
Grant me Your favor;
draw me close to You.

I am wrapped
    in the womb of Your world.
Help me to burst out
    that I may see Your Face
    without the veil.
I know Your Heart-beat,

      I hear Your Voice,
but I yearn to know
    in all detail
    the features of Your Face
and feel directly on my skin
    the touch of Your Skin.
Birth me into Your Presence.
I must first learn to sit with You
before I can learn to stand
    and then begin to walk
      in Your world.
Feed me the food of Your Own Body.
Nurture me, O Lord.

The window frames a view
and light filters through
past the wildflowers on the hill
to wave Your Presence in—
You who care for all of this,
who set the vibration going—
the chain of existence
that began with the word "Be".
As I pull on this chain,
help me to open up each link
    and let it go,
acknowledge it and pass through
    to the next
and the one before
until I come to the lock
    that holds the beginning of Time—

then give me the key
    to turn that pattern
that all the worlds may open
    fully to my sight.

O God,
give me the gift of speech
    in Your Name,
help me to read Your words
    on the tablet of creation.
Help me to translate vision
    into sound
and intimate true feelings
    through the vehicle of voice.
Give me access
    to right insight
that I may offer
    Your bread
    to those who are hungry.
Even from stones,
    bread can come
with just a little of Your Water's Source.
One drop is all it takes.
Help me to distill
    the drop
    that each moment asks
    to make it full of Life—
    Living—
breathing nourishment into need.

It feels like a time of celebration.
It was a liquid summer day
    with heat waves pouring past
    washing me in sweat.
But now the sky has ruptured
    burst with its own grace
and we lift up the corners
    of our aprons, our arms,
        our face
to let fresh water wash us
    and relieve our heat
bringing us into the coolness of Your Rain,
    Lord,
into the Joy of Your Abundant Peace.

No matter how bad it gets,
    there is always meaning in existence,
though sometimes we have to borrow
        a flashlight
in order to see it.

Weave the words,
wind the melodies,
songs of existence
    can always be reborn.

For South Africa

Longing to be free,
    they come,
marching en masse
towards a point that hovers
    above them, before them,
    inside of them . . .
dust rolls off their feet,
and the rhythm of their voices rises
    throbbing the earth,
reawakening the passion it had known
    for centuries,
passion stilled by layering
    of cold colonial ways
erupts hot in the core of the land
and hearts hold each other
    hand to hand,
and look from side to side
    and then straight on—
straight on to freedom.
This rising torrent will not cease
    until the stream is restored
    to the stream-bed
and crops are allowed
    to grow
nurtured by a white and
    a black hand,
        holding together
        one tool.

Blue jay,
visiting this branch,
you are dusted with the same blue
of the delphinium
    regal in the garden,
iridescent in the sun,
startling in your "blueness":
a ray of color
    piercing our world.
"Wake up!"
"Look at me."
Know that color IS—
a manifold gift and a message:
from Oneness comes diversity;
multitudes arise from one seed.
Thousands of lights are lit
    from one candle,
and this universe is ablaze,
    ablaze with meaning,
    with numinosity.
Follow bursts of color
    back to their Source.
Ride the thread of existence
    back to the word "Be".

Straight on 'til morning
    and tens of thousands shall come
until millions move
    deeper,
    deepest

        within themselves,
striking rich ore
mining the haven,
      the words,
that are the source of life's spring.

Guide us to Your giving,
awaken our senses to Your need
      for us in us
which is our need . . .
The seed
      slips through the air
           arcing to earth
      which opens her belly to receive
              pockets
      for paradise to grow.

The firmament—
      across the starry tracks—
          so firm beneath our spirit-feet.
We can follow,
      and run among the brightness,
      the points of almost perfection
      until we come to the point
      of recognizing our own way;
          our own star-self,
and climb back down
      the sky ladder
      to set foot here

  imprinting this earth
    with the sight
      of other worlds.

Happy, busy voices;
  and prism colors
    dance across the floor.
Children helping each other . . .
  what a joy!
"Call me when it's high enough,
  I'll be in my room."
The water fills the tub,
  and then it's full.
Washing off the dirt of the day,
  the dust of work and play . . .
what a gift to have this liquid
  purifier/pure
available for Life—
to wash itself and renew
  these bodies
that carry Love around.

Instruments of many kinds
  live within this space—
drums, saz, piano, rebab,
  even a cuckoo-call . . .

Such cuckoos we are sometimes—
loony-birds who judge ourselves
   and hide
behind rocks of our own making,
forgetting we can fly,
   much less sing.
Lord, open our eyes
   to what lives inside
      us;
split this loony-bird in two
   that the phoenix
   may rise from the center
midst the ashes and tears of passages
whose darkness we will barely remember
when we rise into the light.

Ah! There . . .
I can feel Your fingers
   on my cheek,
caressing my face with Your breeze.
You soothe my skin
and smoothe out the worries,
   the tensions of the day,
and inside myself,
   I can lie down and rest.
You will carry the banner
   while I sleep,
for You have no need to renew—
You, the Ever-Living,

    the Eternal,
    the Restorer to Life,
guide me to Kawthar.

The tough outer shell must first break
to reveal the round nut of forgiveness inside.
No more pointing fingers;
    "no time" has arrived.
Crack that inner shell and fresh milk flows
and we can share the firm white meat—
swallowing together the food of unitedness;
clear milk—no color are we.
We look up and find ourselves
    under a tall tree—
whose green fronds shelter and refresh us
    as it rustles in the wind,
and the ocean is so near—
    Let's dive in!

Phone-lines link spaces
    otherwise so far apart
    except within the beat of the heart
    whose inner ear hears wide . . .
Your voice comes inside
    and reminds me
        to listen . . .

and not to crow too soon.
Be quiet, and send letters
    and soft messages
    into the Unseen
that whispers may return—
    and be received.
So quiet the heart must be
    to hear the subtle echoes
    that wave into each cell
    bringing nourishment
    from within the air.
Colorless, tasteless, odorless,
    it yet holds so much—
    the key to life
    and invigoration;
ever present witness to activation;
encourager of inspiration,
air envelops us and penetrates our walls;
    thank God.

A simple little warbler
splashed black and white,
that he may mingle
    in the darkness and the light
        and not be seen . . .
he hops so close,
    zigzagging through the branches,
    as I sit still,
        perched myself,
    on the handrail.

He has the power to fly,
        though even so small.
Make my wings stronger, Lord,
        that I may fly yet higher,
enlarging my awareness of other worlds,
that I, too, may fly through
        the shadows and the light
                and not be seen.

Envy—it's poison spreads quickly
        and taints everything it touches.
Even the smallest drop of envy is
enough to deaden a whole human being.
Doors shut, curtains come down,
        and visitors are unwelcome.
The owner of the house is absorbed
            somewhere else.
But for one moment just open the sky-light,
and the rain of generosity floods down
        through sleeping rooms and hallways,
            living-room, dining-room, and kitchen,
'til the flood-waters clear out the whole house
        and wave the curtains aside.
After the downpour, the light of the sun pours in;
the house becomes so radiant,
        the doors open of themselves.
Neighbors are beckoned and flock in,
bringing what they have to share,
and the owner of the house stands ready
        to welcome all who come.

Blow me away, Lord,
blow me away with Your words.
I am empty,
but when You speak, Lord, I am full.
Shiver my body,
awaken me with Your Love.
I acquiesce;
I will listen. . .

Whose voice is speaking?
"It is I, Your Lord,
who made you of a bit of nothing (of Alaq)
and have raised you up,
    with My hand.
Strive for the good.
Run even more quickly in this race.
For I cannot tell you
    when your time will come.
You must work hard,
and open to play as well.
Hold your family
    in the palm of your hand
and blow warm, pure breath upon them
to effect a changing of the wind.
Time is short, never long,
    when you reach the midday of life—
work hard,
    open to My words,
        and write.
My blessings will be with you,

       and my love.
Do not fear.
I am God—
       the God of Abraham and
            Moses,
       of Adam, and Noah,
            and Lot,
       of Mary and Elizabeth,
       and John the Baptist,
            and Jesu
       and of Muhammad,
       the father you are coming to recognize.
Do not fear . . .
       but pray and keep yourself pure—
open in thanksgiving,
       and rejoice—
for I am near.

Do not fear—
I can blow all of life around,
but still, in the center,
       I can be found."

Blood pours from an opening in my body,
       but I am well.
Strange miracles of life . . .
       that an apparent misfunction
       is really a fertile sign.
Once recognized,
       one can endure it,

>   with peace of mind—
> the passage will continue . . .
> life will flow.
> Don't worry,
>   for that brings death.
> Open to the living,
>   open to creation, to Life—
> and the swirl of all existence
>   will paint your cheeks red
>   with the rosy glow of the sun's subsistence,
> and round your face
>   with the meat and bread
>   and milk
>   of His giving, the Lord, God.

> I am young . . .
> at times I feel it—
> feel Your strength rush through my blood
> and recognize that I am living,
>   and have abundant life, O God.
> Thank you for all You have bestowed.
> Thank You for the wisdom and insight
>   of Your giving
> which cares for me,
>   yet makes me stretch
>   to come out of my nascent self
>   to awaken and arise in Your bliss—
> How can I not be grateful?
>   You have been so generous,

   and are so generous,
for You are the Most Generous One,
   and the Most Pure.
Thank You, thank You, my Lord,
and forgive my shortcomings
   in implementing Your gifts
    to even better use
     and purposes.
Help me to see more clearly.
Open me to Your Word.
Do unto me as You will Lord,
   for I am clay in Your hands;
but You have breathed spirit into me
   and this spirit I bring
    with both hands,
     offering myself to You.

The storm brings me inside
where I hold close old clothes
and patterned memories,
turning the pages of my heart,
hearing voices of familiar moments
   rising to my ears—
Don't get lost.
  Be brave,
you've lost nothing really.
Nostalgia covers old pain.
Look afresh, and you will see
the shell breaks only to reveal the kernel

        we can eat.
Don't hold on to the husk.
       Enjoy and share the food.

The rain beats on the deck
        drumming,
and my heart begins to dance.
"Look!" my daughter says,
      "Why is it when I pour water on this cloth
it is no longer stiff, but folds and moves?"
Yes, amazing, to change from solid thing
       to flowing beingness,
        able to respond
         to need and new beginnings.
The rain-wind shakes the trees;
      maracas the leaves become,
          augmenting rhythms,
and washed away in this storm,
      I find myself anew.

Words—
  must fit together
        just right—
a necklace strung
     with particular beads—
piece by piece
      until the whole balances in symmetry

and meaning becomes visible
    stone by shell by gem.
May Your meaning continue to be strung
    in wholeness within my heart.

Lord, I yearn to fill the duty You bring—
I yearn to offer myself into Your Hands.
Help me to shake loose of myself,
    to crack this shell that thinks:
"Oh, this is the way it was supposed to be,"
    and keeps itself blind to what is.
Shake me loose, Lord,
    'til the change falls out of my pockets
    and my shoulders relax,
    and my hair falls down—
then maybe I can begin to see, Lord,
    what it was I wanted to hold onto so much.

I wanted to be diligent,
I wanted to "work hard",
but maybe my definitions
    are different from Yours.
You don't work with exclusions—
everything is included
    in Your field of vision,
so to "work hard" encompasses play.
Help me to remember, Lord,

not to be controlled
> by deadlines,
> by diligence,
> by desire,
but when things go awry,
> to stop and listen.
Now, Your message comes through loud and clear—
Take a vacation—take a break—
> and remember who you are.

Work is finished and Your colors call me . . .
I walk down the road to see You better.
Venus lingers in the sky,
> but soon in the Face of Your Radiance,
> I can see her no longer.
A mourning dove calls,
> and then begins a chorus of owls.
The birds know when Your Sun rises,
> how can we humans sleep?
From trees all around, their voices gather in praise
> and I, standing below in my feathered vest,
> watch for a moment as a bird.
Ribbon by ribbon of rose,
Your light rises
> and sky that was no color
> becomes Light-blue.
I step sideways to watch more fully,
> and find a fallen branch at my feet.
Let my old branches fall, too,
that I may stand new in Your sight—

new at the dawn of creation,
new in Your Light.
Just next door,
  a child is waiting to be born—
perhaps this moment,
that new being stirs
  and begins his or her journey
    out into this world.
Your miracles are innumerable.
Every millisecond
  a new atom of being
  takes on Your color
  and becomes
    You.

On the road home,
  bright orange against the green of the maples,
  Turk's cap lilies range wild.
You planted them
  and multiplied them
  and long ago, I carried one home.
So when I return, Your lilies
  will greet me at my doorstep, too.
Good morning, little newt,
  I pass along the way,
echoing the colors of the lilies,
  and the sky—
the orange of God's glory,
  His sunset, and His dawn,
   wash your face and all of you.

The waves,
the ebb and flow—
      the moon is waning,
      but sometimes it is full
      and sometimes it just begins to shine—
the pattern of our existence
      is laid before our eyes.

I left the house at night,
      but now it is day . . .
the ones within the house
      still don't know.
When they arise,
      help me to greet them,
      and wish them well
           on their way.

The phases of the moon—
the phases of my life—
energy swells
      and then recedes.
I soar
      and then slump
into gravity's pull—
let it be . . .
my time will come again,
and I will fly

      split like a seed into the air
      riding the currents, the waves in the sky
until I come to rest
      and plant myself in earth again
      to grow a new body once more,
      a new vehicle for traveling
      through Time and Space.

Sodden, I lie upon this pillow,
      filled with fluids of bodily making,
I hardly have energy to write,
and yet the current trembles
and resonance
      results in movement of my pen.
I awake,
      and sleep again
rocked in the rhythms
      of Your making, Lord,
rocked in the rhythms of Your Love—
      of Your gentle creating, Lord.
I accept, and watch and listen,
and love
      to love You, my Lord.
How can I fight against
      this momentary lackluster shine?
It is of Your giving, Lord,
and though my body lies still,
Your energy somewhat confined
      continues to run
           up and down my spine

and flowing through my heart
        and mind
                and hand
continues through this pen
to search for You,
        to find Your matching Grace,
        to seek, to look for
                everywhere,
                        Your Face.

Listen to the heart
        and act on what you hear.
Don't doubt,
  don't fear—

The morning comes hot and early,
the locusts drone.
Even here in New Jersey,
        nature has her say.
"Summer is coming to a close".
"Listen, and prepare".
Mark the thickening,
        and then the thinning of the air.

The night of power
 comes suddenly.
Only one awake in inner prayer
 will grasp it securely—
through God's Grace,
 and no other,
deliverance comes.
Let go the shaft of daily duty
and grasp the beam of Love.
Love will keep you alert and awake
 watching for a glimpse of the Beloved,
 yearning for just a trace of Holy Perfume.
On the wings of the night
 when it flies highest,
grab hold, and nestle yourself
 behind its neck,
feeling the soft feathers of God's giving,
and listening to the whispers of the stars . . .
"Surely, the Beloved is approaching;
 for in my heart, there is a quickening of Joy."

A snore awakens me,
 and keeps me awake—
this breathing voice
 calls with insistence—
it seems to say,
"Mama, I need you,
 come help me."
Lord, protect my children,
 keep Shams safe.

Whenever a child is missing,
> my body knows.
I cannot rest,
> except in commending
> my children's care to You,
> O Guardian of All—
the Merciful and Compassionate,
guide them safely home.

O Allah,
> Your ways seem to waylay us,
> and then when we least expect it,
> You set us free.
Remind me.
Help me to trust . . .
> to trust the unfolding
> that comes with Your Good Grace.

I wait,
> wait for Your words,
> kneeling now,
on this carpet of green . . .
Lord, God,
> You have many names;
> many faces have brought Your Face close.
Muhammad, Jesus, Buddha,
> and fathers and mothers full of love,

      put a light in the window
      that draws You in.
You see the warmth and the joy of the house,
      and You say,
      "O, yes,
      there is one of my children,
      let me go to his or her aid."
O Lord,
      I await You,
      and my heart is full.

The morning is lightening;
I feel Your breath—
it wraps me in security
and I am grateful
      to come home again.
Thank You for waiting for me,
      for unhinging my fears
that they may fall from me
      like outgrown wings
      that carried me backward into the night.
I come forward now,
      and put my face to Your mirror—
      the whole of creation,
      outside and within,
watching,
to see Your glance
      through my eyes.

It's funny
>	how birds claim their territory—
the crow caws
>	and the blue jay squawbles
>	and flies by
to mark another corner;
>	he calls from there
"I'm here . . .
>	this is my space,
>	these are my berries and fruits."
But the crow still caws forth his claim.
Lord, help us to know how to share,
>	how to dismantle the invisible walls;
to know that unless I feed another,
>	I cannot truly feed myself.

O Lord,
>	draw me into Your side.
Through the wound they made,
>	draw me upward into Isa's heart.
Pain is carried in this world;
>	do not let it be in vain.
From Isa's heart, I can see
>	the multitudes and their misgivings.
Guide them aright, O Lord.
Let fall the doubts,
>	and the javelins of fear.
Bend the swords into handles
>	upon which we can pull
>	and feel Your support.

Don't let mankind go astray.
Let the voice of women, of mothers rise.
One pieta was enough for all of us.
Let us remember.
Let us remember, Lord,
       and give birth to strength that is pure
       and filled with love.

O God,
       I am as nothing in Your hands.
Muhammad heard Your words
       and moved with strength.
Help me not to be misguided,
       and to be steadfast.

Dawn awakens me.
The cool fresh air pulls me alert
       to the coming of light in the sky,
and again I traverse the road
       to Your morning.
I see
       the mist enveloping
       gently swaddling Your creation
and how the mist unfolds
that Your smile may greet Your creatures.
The sun pauses, a red, round, single eye
       at the horizon,

then floats upward, behind a cloud,
but the light of that smiling eye
    cannot be hid.
Its gaze reaches so high and so wide.
Your Light simply Is.
        Everywhere.

A candle burns
    beside "Allah".
The gold script comes to life
    and breathes . . .
and just now
    the sun has risen high enough
to tap upon my window
    with radiant light fingers.
The candle is not ashamed;
    nor does the sun want it to be.

The cicadas roar
    and a few jays call.
Summer is ending.
    Fall and winter approach.
Choose your partner;
    the music stirs;
    the dance will soon begin.
Will envy still accompany you
    through this next season?

Certainty, that is the partner I choose.
Open, listen and hear.
Follow the path of the heart,
    the en-Lightened heart.
Bow in worship and draw near.

Biographical Note

CAMILLE HAMILTON ADAMS HELMINSKI was raised by two wonderful parents, who celebrated with deep spirit the beauty of this magnificent creation yet died early in 1971. She and her husband, Kabir Helminski, were married in 1974 and have raised three beautiful, spirited children, Matthew, Shams, and Cara, for whose presence, and their precious growing families, they are deeply grateful.

Camille has been mentored by a number of very dear souls, and has especially focused within the Mevlevi Tradition of Rumi for more than 35 years. In 1988, Camille and Kabir founded the Threshold Society, a non-profit organization rooted within the traditions of Sufism and dedicated to facilitating the direct personal experience of the Divine. In 1980, they had co-founded Threshold Books in order to bring into English many classic spiritual texts, including some of the first modern translations of Jalaluddin Rumi. As Co-directors of the Threshold Society, she and Kabir continue to teach internationally, deeply inspired by the Light of the Qur'an and the wisdom of the Prophets. She has been a mentor of the Snowmass Interspiritual Dialogue, the Spiritual Paths Foundation (which promotes peace, respect, and mutual understanding between peoples of diverse spiritual traditions through engagement in contemplative practice), and also is recognized as a spiritual elder by WISE (Women's Islamic Initiative of Spirituality and Equality).

She has authored and co-translated many books, including:

Awakened Dreams
Jewels of Remembrance
The Rumi Daybook
Happiness without Death

The Light of Dawn, Daily Readings from the Holy Qur'an

Women of Sufism, a Hidden Treasure, Stories and Writings of Mystic Poets, Scholars, and Saints (which brought to light the integral contribution of women to the spiritual path of Islam)

The Book of Character, Writings on Virtue and Character from Islamic and Other Sources

The Book of Nature, A Sourcebook of Spiritual Perspectives on Nature and the Environment

Rumi's Sun, the Teachings of Shams of Tabriz (from the *Maqalat*)

Rumi and His Friends, Stories of the Lovers of God (from the *Menaqib al-Arifin* of Aflaki)

Camille has embarked on a new series of "Songs of the Soul," books of poetic reflection, that began in 1990 with the inspiration of *Words from the East* and is now further blossoming through several forthcoming publications: *Ramadan Songs of Love, On the Way Home,* and *Exaltations*.

She seeks to encourage all souls to witness the Beauty of this Creation and to share in its preservation through heart to heart connections in recognition of our interwoven interdependence with everything that is—one family of Beingness breathed by our Magnificent Sustainer, no matter what name we may be inspired to use to name that
Source of Life and Loving
that pours
through everything—
may we drink
deeply
and be restored,
rebalanced,
recalibrated
and poured out again
with Love.

www.ingramcontent.com/pod-product-compliance
Lightning Source LLC
Chambersburg PA
CBHW020427010526
44118CB00010B/466